Field Hockey for Beginners

The Ultimate Guide to Mastering Everything from Rules, Sticks, and Etiquette to Ball Control, Shooting, and Goalkeeping

Table of Contents

Introduction

Hockey, a game of originality and unique history, is one of the most popular stick games played worldwide. In this ultimate field hockey guide for beginners, the fundamental techniques to becoming an outstanding player are well introduced and explained in detail. It doesn't matter if you're a complete novice, starting a career as a field hockey player, or expanding your already rich knowledge of the game. This comprehensive guide is your key to unlocking the amazing world of field hockey.

This guide has been crafted with your learning journey in mind. It is engaging and has made learning potential easily accessible, ensuring you'll be equipped with the proper skills and knowledge even if you've never held a hockey stick before. This book covers every basic element of field hockey, from the fundamental rules to ball control, shooting, scoring with accuracy, and goalkeeping strategies. Every aspect and topic is explained concisely and with a hands-on approach.

This book's easy approach to readers is simple and friendly, setting it apart from others. It breaks down what may seem too complex for your understanding into basic, step-by-step instructions, making it easy for a beginner to grasp and practice. It is practical, offering methods that can immediately be applied to a practice field or area. This book further discusses often-overlooked concepts like the power of teamwork and the unique etiquette that makes field hockey a truly wonderful experience.

As you immerse yourself further into the dynamic world of field hockey, be certain this guide lays out a solid foundation of the sport for you. It is your ultimate companion on the journey you're embarking on. So, let the pages ignite your passion and empower you to master every aspect of the game. Good luck, dear reader.

Chapter 1: The Background of Field Hockey

Field hockey is a fast-paced, high-energy sport requiring full mind and body engagement. Two eleven-person teams compete to physically outclass the opposition and strategically outwit them. The sport requires fitness, agility, and hand-eye coordination, so your full presence is required on the field to be successful. Field hockey is a fun, social activity that creates strong interpersonal bonds and provides much-needed cardio-based exercise.

1. Field hockey is a perfect sport for all genders and ages. Source: https://www.pexels.com/photo/group-of-woman-playing-on-green-field-during-daytime-163526/

Field hockey is perfect for both genders and all ages. The sport is easy to learn and difficult to master, so you will always have a goal of improvement to work toward. The sport's physical demand is great for pushing your body to its limits. The crack of the hockey stick meeting the ball sends it zipping across the field, giving you goosebumps and filling you with excitement. As a beginner in field hockey, there is so much to learn that this hobby can easily facilitate obsessive dedication. Grab your stick and a ball and get ready for the reward of playing field hockey.

Jump into this fulfilling journey as you tap into the basics and learn the intricacies of this magnificent sport. To understand field hockey, you must grasp the sport's fundamentals, be familiar with the equipment and the necessary gear, and understand the game's rules and objectives. With this rudimentary knowledge, you can step onto the field with enough understanding to participate. This background knowledge allows you to determine which position your skillset is best suited for. You can build on more skills and become proficient enough to compete comfortably from this foundation.

Understanding the Basics of Field Hockey

Field hockey is played on a field of grass or on artificial turf. The fast-paced game is played by two competing teams of eleven. One player is the goalkeeper, and the other players compete in different positions on the field. The game's objective is to score more goals than your opponents by hitting the ball with the hockey stick into the net. Whoever scores more goals before the time runs out is the winner. Hockey matches are typically one hour long, divided into four quarters of 15 minutes. A match will end in a win, a loss, or a draw.

The sport is played on a 100 by 60-yard field with eleven players or less in the game at any time. Field hockey requires much strategy and collaboration. Therefore, each player has a unique function. Different formations are used depending on the team's skill set. You can play with three defenders and five midfielders or three defenders, four midfielders, and three forwards. Each formation has pros and cons. Coaches often switch up the formations according to the opposition team's characteristics. Although hockey is highly physical, the game's mental aspects are equally important. Therefore, ultimate focus is required on the pitch to observe the game strategically unfolding while adjusting and using your physicality to its fullest.

The five-man positions in field hockey are the goalkeeper, the sweeper, defenders, midfielders, and forwards. The goalkeeper stays in the net because their main objective is to stop goals from being scored. The sweeper is in front of the defenders and behind the midfielders. The sweeper's main objective is to defend the goal. Some players stay back and fulfill the defensive role. The midfielders are the playmakers who switch between offense and defense depending on the game's requirements. The forwards are in front and are focused on offensive play. The forwards' main objective is to score goals.

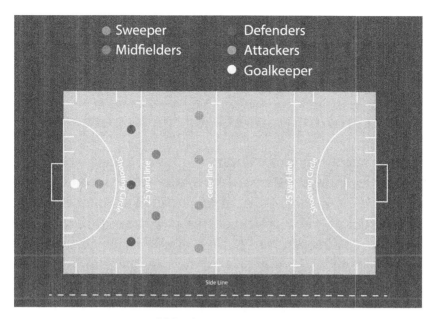

2. *Field hockey positions. Source:*
https://cdn.shopify.com/s/files/1/0653/2186/1366/files/field-
hockey-player-positions.jpg?v=1667566572

The ball is passed between players, or a player can run and dribble the ball to either side of the field. If one team is in possession of the ball, they will push forward and attempt to score a goal, while the other team tries to retrieve the ball by tackling a player or intercepting the ball. Field hockey is not a contact sport, so you are not allowed to grab or push players to get the ball. Although field hockey is not considered a contact sport, the sticks and hard ball, coupled with the game's physicality and pace, make it a dangerous sport. The rules of the game must be followed to minimize injuries, but it is common to get cut, bruised, or even to break bones, like in many other sports.

The umpire governs the game with a whistle and a simple system of cards, commands, and hand signs. When a green card is issued, a player must leave the field for two minutes. A yellow card means a player must leave the field for five minutes, and a red card means the player is banned from the rest of the game. The ref watches carefully to declare fouls and call goals.

Equipment and Gear for Beginners

The two main pieces of equipment in field hockey are the ball and stick. Hockey sticks are made from wood, carbon, fiberglass, or a mixture of these composite materials. The hockey stick is the most expensive piece of equipment other than the goalkeeper kit. A high-quality stick is important because it will last longer and reduce the shock on your hands when the ball impacts with the stick. A field hockey ball is made of solid plastic, not easily broken or damaged. Players must wear specialized shoes with short studs, enabling better grip while running. Professional field hockey is mostly played on artificial turf but is commonly played on grass, especially in amateur and school leagues.

3. *Field hockey stick, ball, and shoes. Source:*
https://www.rawpixel.com/image/9653757/image-person-public-domain-man

The goalkeeper has more equipment than the outfield players because the position puts you in the line of fire of a rock-hard ball. The danger a goalkeeper faces necessitates additional safety requirements. The goalkeeper wears a helmet with a protective face mask. In addition to a helmet, they wear elbow pads, neck and chest protection, foot protectors, gloves, and leg guards. When a forward shoots at the net, the ball can whizz toward the goalkeeper up to a speed of 100 mph. The goalkeeper needs this protective gear to stay safe. It contributes to the unique role a goalkeeper plays in field hockey. Unlike other players, goalkeepers can touch the ball with any part of the body, whereas outfield players can only use their sticks. However, the goalkeeper's mobility is limited by the excess gear they wear.

4. Field hockey goalkeeper. Source:
https://commons.wikimedia.org/wiki/File:Hockey_keeper.jpg

Although not as excessive as the goalkeeper's safety equipment, outfielders also have safety requirements.

Players run at full speed, and the ball moves incredibly fast, so the risk of injury is high. Therefore, players must wear shin and mouth guards. The shin guards provide leg and ankle protection should you get struck with a stick or ball. Protecting your body is important, but field hockey players look after their hockey sticks seriously. Specialized tapes are available to bandage hockey sticks to prevent them from getting damaged in the heat of competition. A hockey bag is not required, but it is a useful piece of equipment. They have space for your stick, balls, and pockets for your kit.

Rules and Objectives of the Game

When playing field hockey, several complicated rules are involved, but once you get into the game, it becomes easier to understand the rules. The main objective is to score goals. The field is divided into four sections. At each end of the field, a semi-circle surrounds the goalposts. These semi-circles are called the "scoring circle" and colloquially referred to as the "D." You can only score a goal when in the scoring circle. The ball can't be hit higher than a player's knees from anywhere on the field except inside the scoring circle. The rule of hitting the ball at any height in the scoring circle is why goalkeepers wear so much protective gear.

5. A field hockey field looks similar to a soccer field. Source: Brieuc Verstreken, CC BY-SA 4.0 <https://creativecommons.org/licenses/by-sa/4.0>, via Wikimedia Commons: https://commons.wikimedia.org/wiki/File:European_field_hockey _championship_stadium_in_Antwerp,_Belgium_2019.jpg

A field hockey stick is curved at the end, flat on one side, and rounded on the other. You are only allowed to hit the ball with the flat side of the curve. Players can move by passing or dribbling the ball along the field. Outfield players are not allowed to touch the ball with any parts of their body other than the hockey stick, or a foul is called. When a foul is called, the opposing team gets a free hit. A free hit is also awarded when the ball exits the sideline, a boundary drawn around the field. A penalty stroke is awarded if a foul is committed inside the scoring circle. A penalty stroke is when one player takes a free shot at the goal, and the goalkeeper attempts to block the shot.

Players run back and forth on the field, passing the ball to one another and attempting to score a goal. The game is only halted when the umpire blows their whistle to make a call. An obstruction rule occurs when the player with the ball uses their body to shield the ball from the opponent attempting to tackle them. Your opponent must be given a fair opportunity to take the ball from you with their stick without you blocking their attempt with your body.

Chapter 2: Getting Started: Field Hockey Fundamentals

Now that you have a basic understanding of field hockey's rules and objectives, you must learn some of the game's fundamentals. Holding the stick and swinging wildly at the ball is not a formula for success. The basics of footwork, body positioning, passing, and gripping your hockey stick can save you from mid-match embarrassment. More importantly, grasping the fundamentals can prevent unnecessarily hurting yourself and others. Safety comes before competition because it is the only way to ensure everyone has a good time on the pitch.

Controlling your body and equipment opens a grocery list of decisions you can make on the field. Hockey is such a dynamic team sport due to numerous strategies that can be explored to win. The key aspects of the sport will be used throughout the years you compete. You will get more advanced as you practice, but these fundamentals will remain relevant. Advanced playing techniques are built on the backbone of understanding the fundamentals as a foundation for your playing style.

The basic tricks you learn will create the unique game puzzle you play as an individual competitor. You will develop favorite techniques and sowing combinations that will dazzle you. The basics are the building blocks weaved to take a beginner to an advanced level. Everybody has to start somewhere. As you compete as a newcomer to field hockey, your primary focus should be mastering the basics. Many of the game's rules can be learned as you compete, while the fundamentals must be internalized and learned by heart long before you set foot into a competition.

Proper Grip and Stick Handling

The stick is the main tool of a field hockey player. Without a hockey stick, you cannot compete. The hockey stick is used in many ways. The different shots and passes you can make require shifting the hand's positioning on the grip. Some hand positions are more common than others. Properly gripping your hockey stick gives you more control of the ball and more power. A proper grip allows you to tackle opponents and intercept passes more easily.

The hockey stick has different sections you must be aware of to play effectively. The grip is at the top of the stick and covered with suede, leather, or a similar material. The shank, or the handle of a hockey stick, is the long, flat, uncovered section extending from the grip to the head. At the bottom of the stick is the head, the start of the curve at the end of the stick. The heads vary according to a player's style or comfort. The toe is the rounded tip at the end of the stick, and the heel connects the handle to the toe. Imagine your hockey stick's head as a foot. The toes are at the end, and the heel is connected to your leg. Similarly, the stick's toe is at the end, and the heel is connected to the handle. The flat part of your stick's head is called the face.

6. *The flat part of the stick is called the face. Source: No machine-readable author provided. NilsKruse assumed (based on copyright claims)., CC BY-SA 3.0 <http://creativecommons.org/licenses/by-sa/3.0/>, via Wikimedia Commons: https://commons.wikimedia.org/wiki/File:Indoor_hockey_stick2.jpg*

The basic grip is achieved by placing your right hand at the top of the hockey stick and your left hand at the bottom of the grip. Your hand should be wrapped around the stick so that your index finger and thumb touch. This grip is used most because it allows you to pass and receive the ball, dribble, and maneuver easily. This grip may initially feel uncomfortable because you will not be accustomed to it. However, when you settle into play, you will quickly get used to it. The grip will cause you to bend down so that you are always ready for the ball.

Basic Footwork and Body Positioning

Once you are used to holding the stick correctly, you must focus on your body and foot positioning. The ball is on the ground most of the time, so you will almost always be in a lowered posture. One way to be more comfortable being close to the ground and having more control of your movements is by spreading your legs widely. When your legs are spread, you are automatically closer to the ground. There will be a slight bend in your knees when taking this wide-legged stance.

Field hockey moves quickly, so your body positioning and stick holding must be geared toward reacting fast. Field hockey balls travel at astounding speeds, and the player positions shift dynamically throughout the match to create space and openings. Therefore, as a hockey player, you must always be ready to spring into action. Remaining light on your feet and constantly moving allows you to keep your senses tuned in. The connection between your body and mind is strengthened by consistently moving to be aware of your muscles and positioning. Being caught flat-footed is a sin on the hockey field.

Field hockey is a sport requiring high athleticism. Therefore, doing basic running and agility drills will be helpful. Many injuries can be avoided when you train your body to respond well to explosive movements. The sport has many stop-and-start movements, from standing still to full sprints. Furthermore, the nature of dribbling means moving swiftly from side to side. Therefore, approach field hockey like any sport, requiring a lot of running to train your athleticism before you train your skills. Being in touch with your body mechanics and balance is a huge advantage in field hockey.

You must move your feet according to where you are moving or where you want to position the ball. Be mindful of where you place your feet in relation to the ball. For example, when making a long pass, you will step ahead of the ball and drag your stick across your body. Your footwork in field hockey should always be pre-determined and deliberate. How you move your feet dictates if you are in the best position to pull off the passes, shots, or blocks.

As mentioned, the obstruction rule does not permit a player to block the ball with their body. Therefore, always be aware of your body positioning to prevent fouls. Also, you cannot touch the ball with your feet. Positioning your feet according to the anticipated move prevents other body parts from coming into contact with the ball, minimizing fouls. The key to footwork and body positioning is to think ahead and know where you are about to move and where you currently are.

Introduction to Passing and Receiving Techniques

Field hockey is a team sport. All the plays are woven together by passing and receiving. Passing and trapping are the first two techniques you must learn to become a competent field hockey player. The most basic pass is the push pass. With your standard grip, one hand at the top of the stick and the other at the bottom of the grip, drag the ball along the ground, building momentum to send it forward. The same movement is used for basic dribbling. Run, rolling the ball against the stick's face along the ground in one motion. The ball never loses contact with your hockey stick in this basic dribbling technique. To pass the ball, roll it along the ground and push it into the ball to send it to the intended position with kinetic energy.

7. Pass the ball using kinetic energy. Source: https://pixabay.com/photos/hockey-competition-ball-athlete-3335416/

Receiving the ball, or trapping, is the next skill to help you become a proficient field hockey team member. The two basic trapping techniques are a hard hand trap and a soft hand trap. The hard hand trap is when you stiffen your hands with your stick on the ground to receive a pass. Hold your stick diagonally to trap the ball and bring it to a complete stop. The soft hand trap receives the ball using a motion across your body. Allow the ball to roll across your body, slowing down the momentum, but do not bring the ball to a complete stop. This soft hand trap allows you to use the ball's motion to your advantage and control your body movement with the ball's direction.

Trapping, passing, and dribbling are methods for creating movement along the field. Creative passing opens space so you and your teammates can find holes in the opposition's defense. Calling for the ball and looking for open players while running into position is how passing and trapping are used effectively. Practicing passing with a few people can help you understand the ball's movement and become familiar with operating your hockey stick.

Practice is essential for passing and receiving the ball. You become accustomed to field hockey physics when you repeatedly hit and trap the ball. There are different ways to strike the ball, with varying grips and stick positioning. You can intuit some of the passing and trapping techniques once you've hit the ball around enough. Researching will only help you a little in the beginning. You will improve by getting onto the turf with a stick and a ball. Practicing passing is a great way to get used to the game because the stakes are not as high as in a match, and you become accustomed to how the ball moves and reacts when impacting your stick.

Chapter 3: Mastering Ball Control

Controlling the ball on the hockey field is called dribbling. Dribbling goes beyond merely controlling the ball. It uses the hockey stick to create short strokes and moves the ball to the alternate side, left and right, of your body while moving on the field. While moving the ball skillfully, you're simultaneously fleeing from defenders attempting to snatch the ball from you. Dribbling is an essential skill you must possess as an effective player on the hockey field. In dribbling, you run in the opposite direction of the field to score a goal, playing the ball through defenders. When dribbling, swiftness and precision are essential for running with the ball. Possessing these skills is usually difficult for a beginner, so you must master controlling the ball from scratch.

To become excellent at ball control, you must first know the basics, develop and grow your dribbling skills, learn to navigate the field confidently, and keep practicing ball control through consistent drills and games. This chapter explains the basics of dribbling and how to master ball control. Prepare your mind, as you'll get a full pack of content to help you understand field hockey.

Developing Dribbling Skills

Dribbling is essential in any field sport, including hockey. Therefore, you must master it. How do you master ball control? Similar to how anyone becomes successful at anything, dribbling requires constant practice and good techniques if you want to master it. Dribbling demands touching the ball and not losing control and stamina. You must be able to run fast at a comfortable pace. Begin by lightly hitting the ball each time just a few feet to successfully control the ball while running at a fast pace on the field. Starting on a light note, you can master walking and hitting your ball before jogging while hitting the ball. Gradually advance to running while hitting the ball when you've successfully mastered the initial skills.

Several strategies to develop your dribbling skills are imbibed in the dribbling types. Knowing these strategies, you can properly channel your techniques and energy according to game rules.

Dribbling Techniques

Knowing general dribbling techniques is necessary before shedding more light on the dribbling types. These techniques are:

1. Bend your knees a little and place the ball in front of you.

2. To have the correct hold on the stick, straighten your posture and place a hand at the top and one at the bottom.

3. To tap the ball on each side, turn the hook of the stick.

4. Push the ball while walking forward.

Now you know the general techniques to play or master hockey dribbling movement, here are dribbling techniques:

Straightforward Dribbling

__8.__ Straightforward dribbling technique. Source: https://fitness365.me/wp-content/uploads/2021/06/aid9728-v4-728px-Play-Field-Hockey-Step-8-Version-4.jpg

You must first master the basic hockey stance before using straightforward dribbling. Apply the following tips for an accurate stance.

1. Bend your knees but make sure your posture is straight.

2. Place your hands at the top and bottom of the hook.

3. While the ball is in front of you, put your right foot forward and tap the ball toward the space in front of your left foot.

4. Immediately, meet the moving ball on the left, tapping it with your hook upside down.

5. Repeat as you move forward, moving the ball in opposite directions.

Always keep your eyes up so that you know who to pass it to and the direction needed for that pass. The aim is for a smooth, clean goal in the opposite direction.

Indian Dribbling

9. *Indian dribbling. Source: https://fitness365.me/wp-content/uploads/2020/06/dr.png*

Indian dribbling has existed since the 1956 Olympics game and is one of the best techniques in field hockey. When you master it, you're sure to become a star yourself. When this dribbling is used properly, your opponents cannot tell your next move, left or right, while you play at a high speed. It is best performed in a solitary stance.

1. Spread out your legs, each should be adjacent to the width of your shoulders.

2. Straighten your back and keep your knees slightly bent while having your hands firmly placed on the handle.

3. Moving from in front of your left to your right toe, move the ball while dragging it.

4. Flip the hook over and keep doing the same move while moving with the ball.

Apply this technique when you become proficient in dribbling routines.

One-Hand Dribbling

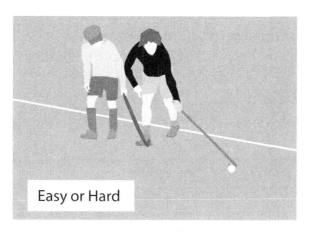

10. One-hand dribbling. Source:
https://i.ytimg.com/vi/Kx42zmXe_0k/maxresdefault.jpg

This technique allows you the freedom to focus on pacing, sprinting, and keeping defenders at bay. Do you have a strong wrist and good hands for turns and twists? Then, this dribbling technique is certainly for you. The one-hand dribbling requires speed and proficiency, meaning you must have mastered the basic dribbling skill to advance to this technique. It is suited for play on the wings. Run with an outstretched arm with the stick in your other hand while you close the ball with the hook.

While dribbling, you must place your ball in the proper position. It mustn't be too far away, or you'd lose control of the ball, and it mustn't be too close to avoid being unable to see the players around you to pass the ball properly. The ball should not be close to your feet, so you don't step or kick it while playing. It's necessary to master these little hockey habits of dribbling the ball correctly so that it becomes natural and easy.

Navigating the Field with Confidence

You can almost tell a losing team from a winning team even before the end of a game. The losing team is those with down faces and shoulders, an aura of gloom, and terrible negative body language. Yes, that's the losing team. Sadly, every game must have a loser, but that doesn't mean the best efforts weren't put in. Feeling nervous in and out of the game is okay, but there are ways to carry yourself no matter your position.

As a beginner, participating in a game filled with unfamiliar players could keep you on the tense edge. If you lack confidence while on the pitch, the most essential thing you must do is to avoid the negatives such as being face down, having sad eyes, and sloppy shoulders. Here are tips to stir up your confidence and posture:

- **Fake the Confidence Until You Feel It**

This phrase might sound familiar. In this case, it can be applied. Even when you feel anxious and fearful of the opposing team, instead of succumbing to your emotions and allowing your body language to follow the beat, hold your head high and keep your chest up with your shoulders back. Affirm yourself by saying, *"You own this pitch. You will give your best, and nothing will make you feel otherwise."*

- **Don't Dwell on Your Mistakes**

Are there any sports where mistakes aren't inevitable? Of course not. No one plays an entirely perfect game, so own your mistakes because they're normal. If you mess up or miss a shot, relax, take a deep breath, and move on mentally. Remember to keep a positive body language at all times.

- **Work on Breathing Techniques if You Feel Pressured**

Sometimes, things will speed up and become too much for your pace. Take a deep breath and slowly work on taking control when the match starts. Slowly inhale and breathe through your nose while your stomach expands and contracts.

Practicing Ball Control

Practicing ball control in field hockey with little experience and few resources regarding spacing and a good instructor is challenging. However, keep up your game and start where you are. Refine your skills by keeping up with field hockey drills that have been tried and tested for years. There is a shooting circle and a neutral zone on the field. As a player, you will always have a defender marking you, so you must creatc cnough room to play the ball without it getting stolen or intercepted by the defender. Drills help you build agility and speed, which will help you move forward. Follow these guidelines for your drills.

1. Setting Up Your Drilling Yard

For this exercise, you'll need two sets of cones, 1 and 5 thirty feet apart, 2 and 4 thirty feet away from the first. Then 3, ten feet away from 1 and 5.

2. The Drill

Start at cone 1, dribbling the ball, sprint to 2, and cut to 3 before pulling the ball around 4. Dribble to 5, then cut around and finish back to 1. Remember to set a timer for each drill and do this as often as possible to increase your speed and improve your cutting-edge technique.

In field hockey, controlling the ball by moving it in an alternate direction is called dribbling. Dribbling is an essential skill you must possess to improve your speed and agility as a player. You must always use the proper stance in dribbling to control the ball and know where your team players are. You learned to navigate the field in confidence. As a beginner or regular player expanding your techniques, you can sometimes face anxiety when first attempting this skill. It is normal, but as you apply the techniques detailed in this chapter, you will overcome your fear.

Chapter 4: The Art of Shooting and Scoring

The concept of shooting and scoring in field hockey are like two sides of a coin, intertwined yet distinct. Technically, a game is won when one team successfully scores more points than the opposing side. Hockey is similar to football in scoring points. It is one point per goal, and only one player can score each point. Therefore, you must learn to practice and improve your shooting techniques to become a master at scoring. You're advantageous to your teammates when your shooting ability is highly efficient. In several hockey drills, about 75% of training sessions are dedicated to practicing shooting, proving that the need to master shooting cannot be overemphasized. Several shooting techniques, like push passes, slap shots, drives, flicks, and scoops, can be amazing attacks on the opposing team.

This chapter explores the different shots in field hockey and the accurate shooting techniques to apply in any position. Also, you'll learn the key strategies for goalkeeping. It is one thing to know shooting techniques and another to defend your team's stand. As a beginner, you can start easily. There is no pressure, and you do not need to practice with opponents if you are not ready. As you dive further into this chapter, prepare your mind for a clearer understanding of what shooting and scoring entail in hockey.

How Points Are Made in Hockey

You score a goal when you successfully hit the ball into the opposing team's net across the line within 16 yards. When there's a penalty, all players in the defending team must line up before their goal line. When the ball is played, a teammate must stop the ball before the ball lands within their opposition's goalposts.

A player is entitled to one point when they score a goal. The official scoreboard records your scores and will indicate an assist (the amount of points gained by a player passing the ball to the goal scorer). A team's wins and losses make up these records. When a player scores three goals in a game, it is called a hat trick.

Shot Types in Field Hockey

Every player's dream is to score as many goals as possible and take the lead in a match. While this is a wonderful dream, to help ease your team's confidence levels, you must first learn how to shoot, starting from the basics. In field hockey, there are 5 major shot types. You can start with any shot, but you must first know what they are and how to apply them. They are as follows:

Drive Shots

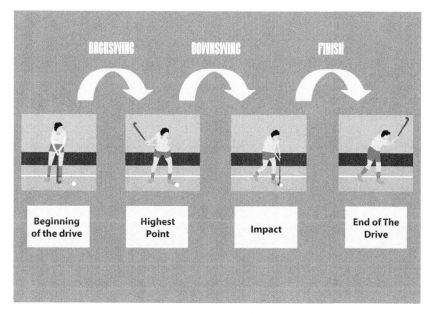

11. The drive shot. Source:
https://www.researchgate.net/publication/23307537/figure/fig1/
AS:601633725612039@1520452066274/Schematic-description-of-
field-hockey-drive-movement.png

This is one of the most common shots. It requires tightly gripping your hockey stick's handle with both hands. Take a fast backswing from this position to shoot the ball. This shot can travel a long way when done correctly. It isn't entirely necessary and suitable for all occasions, but you can apply this shot when making a long pass, a free hit, or a hard shot at the goal. Here are the steps to help you make accurate shots:

1. Ensure your feet are placed together, the ball a few steps in front of you.

2. Place your hands a few inches from the top of the stick's handle. Ensure both hands are not too far apart like you would with a baseball bat.

3. Step toward the ball and swing your stick to strike a shot.

4. Ensure you keep your wrist supple and not firm before striking the ball to yield a powerful shot.

5. Repeat these steps until you get the hang of it.

Slap Shots

12. The slap shot. Source: https://d3i71xaburhd42.cloudfront.net/4dd2b2446f3af03090e16e0 bb4dc94f53ea196c1/1-Figure1-1.png

Unlike the drive that takes a full backswing, the slap shot only needs a half backswing with your hands 8 inches apart on the handle. You can use this technique for shooting or passing the ball and controlling the shots you intend to play. Here are the steps to get accurate shots:

1. Grip the stick slightly with your body perpendicular to the goal post.

2. Set your hands apart, one beneath and the other on the handle, like you would during a dribbling position.

3. Your feet must be placed shoulder-width apart.

4. Place the ball a few inches away from you.

5. Swing your stick toward the ball and into the air.

6. While you swing to hit the ball, leave the stick open toward the end to get some lift on it.

7. To get a more accurate shot, strike the ball with the neck of the stick (the thickest part of the handle just above the heel), keeping it low and pointed toward your target.

Push Passes

13. Push pass. Source:
https://media.sportplan.net/thumbnail/viewer/movies/hockey/Ho
c31/a.png

This shot does not require a backswing. The only catch is that your body strength must be good enough to take the shot. You will need to work on building your muscles and agility to put this technique into practice. The lack of backswing makes it unpredictable. Hence, the player must correctly aim for the post when scoring a good goal.

All you need is a flexible body, a little flicking of your wrist, and boom. The ball's on its way to freedom. Besides scoring, players typically use the push to pass the ball to their teammates while playing. Here are the steps for accurate shots:

1. Place both hands on the stick as in a normal field game, with the left hand at the top and the other at the middle.

2. Your body should be placed perpendicularly to your target point, with your chest facing the ball.

3. Keep your knees bent and let your weight fall to the back of your leg.

4. Ensure the ball isn't near you. The closer it is to you, the less likely you are to spot an opponent in front of you.

5. Keep your wrist soft while you release the ball.

Flick Shots

14. The flick shot is a complex technique. Source:
https://static.toiimg.com/photo/msid-95659363/95659363.jpg

These are quick and solid shots used mostly for scoring. It is a complex technique also used to dodge defenders. You can flick the ball into the air to play it over your opponent's stick. To apply this method, you must be flexible with your stick movement and know how to tilt the stick's hook at a certain angle to get it under the ball and then flick your wrist to get the ball in the air. With constant practice, you'll do this in a short time. Here are the steps for accurate flicking shots:

1. For a flick shot, you must count your steps while moving each leg with the ball. You may have a longer distance to drag it before applying the flick.

2. Cross your legs over each other as you drag the ball forward.

3. Bend your knees as if crouching to help you perform a spring movement.

4. Spread your hands on the stick's handle, allow the ball to roll to the stick's head, and then strike.

5. Your shoulders should remain firm and flat throughout this technique. You can rotate other parts of your body, but not your shoulders.

Scoops

15. Scoop technique. Source:
https://cdn.silverskatefestival.org/1667029416049.jpg

Like the flick technique, scoops also entail lifting the ball into the air but, in this case, a shorter distance. It is used to play a free hit and dodge your opponent's stick. Here are the steps to get accurate scoop shots:

1. Your hands must be kept apart on the stick's handle.

2. Tilt the stick so it's standing parallel to your right arm, like a 90° angle between your left arm and your stick.

3. Decide on your target.

4. Bend your knees and avoid back swinging. Instead, lift the ball into the air.

Understanding Goalkeeping Strategies

Goalkeeping is the last line of defense from an opposing strike in field hockey. With a good goalkeeper, you have an edge, even if the odds are not in your favor. Here are factors you must know to understand good goalkeeping strategies:

- To be a good goalkeeper, you must have good reflexes and balanced stamina. You can improve your stamina by carrying out cardio exercises. Carry out quick drills for your feet or hand-eye coordination for your reflexes.

- You must be swift in making split-second decisions, like predicting other players' likely moves or positions on the field.

- You must maintain good communication with your teammates. You should be good at giving and receiving signals concerning the ball's direction.

- Have good hand-eye coordination. You must be prepared to defend an incoming strike with your stick or block it with any part of your body.

Shooting and scoring are the most crucial aspects of a field hockey game. It is the essence of the game. You must master shooting properly and accurately to score. You can master several shooting techniques to perfect scoring, but first, you must start with the basics. It may be complex to understand all the techniques at once as a beginner, but once you begin, you can gradually progress. Spend more time perfecting your shots because, with the right shot, you can lead and ultimately win a game. You can be a pro in this field. All it takes is practice and consistency. Remember, you're not a winner until you win, so good luck.

Chapter 5: Defensive Strategies for Beginners

Like other sports, your defensive strategy can make all the difference in field hockey. Good defending helps your team maintain control over the game and prevents opposing teams from scoring. Most people believe a strong offense automatically guarantees a win. However, you are as strong as your defense. In field hockey, the defense comprises a goalkeeper, a right and left defender and a center defender. The defenders are charged with feeding the midfielders and the offensive line with the ball.

This chapter discusses marking and tackling basics, how to position and defend as a team, and how to clear the ball from defensive areas during a game.

Marking and Tackling Basics

Marking is the primary defensive technique in field hockey. It can be used throughout the field but is mostly deployed in the defensive zone during a game. This strategy enables you to mark opposing players from the defensive zone.

Zone Defense

This is a defensive strategy where a player covers a specific area in the defensive zone. All team members must be organized and disciplined for this strategy to work. If one area of the zone breaks down, your defense would be breached. When the area of the defense begins to become overcrowded, this is a major setback. The players that are playing defense will begin to feel the heat and could end up with a 2 to 1 situation.

Man-to-Man Marking

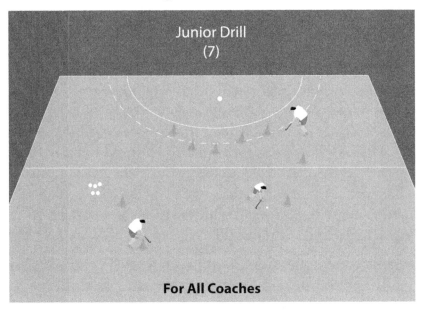

16. Man-to-man marking drill. Source:
https://i.ytimg.com/vi/JnjpHDkoSAw/hq720.jpg?sqp=-
oaymwEhCK4FEIIDSFryq4qpAxMIARUAAAAAGAElAADIQjoAgKJ
D&rs=AOn4CLDPx6uztbC-T-sj8t7urWSXVMlR5A

In this position, a defense player chooses a player in the attacking position to mark. What the defender needs to do here is stay ball side and goal side to block the other team's goal attempts by getting the ball. It's important to note that players need to be a stick's distance away, with the attention on the ball rather than the player. Players usually use confusing stick work to throw the other team off, and this is why it's best to keep an eye on the ball itself.

Mark-Up Zone

It is the most productive defensive strategy. This strategy entails each defensive player having a specific zone and marks any player in that zone. This strategy limits the threat of the opposing attacking player around the ball by stopping a played shot.

Tackling

Tackling is a defensive player's movement to get the ball off an opposing attacking player. You are only allowed to tackle the ball and not the opposing player. A field tackle is like a side tackle in soccer. You aim to dispossess the attacking player using your stick without touching the player. You must be precise to execute a proper tackle. You must know when to go in for the tackle, or it might result in a foul. You can use the block tackle or jab tackle when dispossessing the opposing player.

It doesn't matter which sport you are playing. The mechanism for defending remains the same, whether it's basketball, soccer, or field hockey. You must exploit the attacking players' weak spots or guide them to your strong side. Then, keep tabs on the opposing attacking player until the precise moments when you dispossess them. Mostly, this is done with a loose touch by the attacking player, and you are right on time to jab or block the ball. Remember, your timing must be right.

Position

Knowing how to position yourself to the ball is the first place to begin when marking. Position yourself between the opposing player and the goal or between the opposing player and the ball. The objective is to get to the ball before the opposing player and stop them from having a shot at getting a goal.

When you tilt your face away from the goal, you will be better positioned to defend your goal and clear a ball from the defensive zone. Position yourself at least a stick's distance from the attacking player so you can defend against them and be in the right place for possible interceptions and unexpected passes.

Team Defense and Positioning

A field hockey team comprises 11 players categorized into three groups of field players; the goalkeeper, the defenders and midfielders, and the striker.

Among these three groups are players with distinct positions playing different roles. Field hockey follows the same formation strategies as soccer, basketball, or baseball. These formations enable players to function within a strategic pattern, such as 3-4-3, 4-3-3, or 3-5-2.

The first line in these formations comprises the attackers, the second line consists of the midfielders, and the third line is the defenders. The 3-4-3 formation comprises three attackers, four midfielders, and three defenders. The 4-3-3 formation strategy comprises four attackers, three midfielders, and three defenders.

It doesn't matter whether it is indoor or outdoor hockey. What guides your position is the formation your team executes for a particular game. As a player, you must adjust your role regardless of your position as the game changes before you.

The Strikers (Forward Position): These are the team's offensive weapons. Their responsibility is to harass the opposing defenders' goalkeeper and score goals.

The Midfielders (Midfield Position): These are the middlemen between the striker and defenders. Their position is in the middle of the field, and their responsibility is to defend and attack, often called the engine room, because of their dual roles. They detect the flow and tempo of the game.

The Defenders (Defending Position): These are the last line of defense and a vital part of any sport. They shield the goalkeeper and the goal from the opposing attacking players. They are like stumbling blocks for the opposing team's attackers. The defenders prevent the opposing teams from creating scoring opportunities for their attackers. Additionally, they are tasked with getting the ball across to the midfielders and the strikers.

Goalkeepers: They are an integral aspect of any formation as they help keep the defense against opposing attackers. A goalkeeper's role goes beyond keeping the opposing attackers from scoring. They coordinate the defenders to harass opposing attackers. The goalkeeper should be fast and agile and can use any body part to prevent the ball from entering the goal. Goalkeepers must be fast on their feet to clear the ball from the 'D' area and, with their hands, to keep the opposition shots from entering the goalposts.

Clearing the Ball from Defensive Areas

Knowing how to clear the ball from defensive areas is vital as it enables your team to move from a defensive to an offensive play, giving your team control of the game.

Evaluating the Situation on the Ground: Before clearing the ball from defensive areas, examine the field to see where your teammates, open passing lanes, and the opposing players are positioned. This assessment guides your decision on the right clearance technique.

Using Clearance Technique: If you are a good dribbler, move the ball out of the defensive area by keeping it close to your stick and dribble out of the defensive area. You can use an aerial pass to hit the ball from your defensive zone down the field. This approach moves the ball over the opposing players effectively. Look for an area where your teammates are or you can easily reach them, then swing your stick under the ball to produce a backspin as you direct its movement to your teammates.

Additionally, clear the ball by hitting it over a long distance, striking or pushing it to a teammate in a better position using the flat side of your stick.

Practice: You must work on your dribbling, passing, timing, and hitting skills to clear the ball effectively in a game. It instills confidence when you can easily clear the ball from defensive areas during a game.

Communication: For your team to be effective and get the winning result, you must know how to communicate with each other. Communicate with your teammates when you want to clear the ball and let them know where you are sending it. You could use a hand gesture or non-verbal communication that only your teammates understand.

Body Position: When your stance is low and balanced, you can easily control and clear the ball even under duress from opposing attackers.

Defensive strategies are a major aspect of field hockey. They are integral to a team's success. Having the right team spirit and being one-minded cannot be overemphasized. So, as a defender, you must work with your teammates to ensure your team comes out on top. Remember, the best offense is a good defense.

Chapter 6: Game Play and Strategy

In hockey, there are different strategies and tactics for winning. While you develop your hockey skills, you'll learn it takes more than playing the game to win. You need a plan, good communication with your teammates, and knowing how to implement several tactics to the advantage of your team. The line between winning and losing depends on every player becoming exceptional individually. When you become a skillful player, you won't need to master every tactic to become a great player.

To have these qualities, you must first understand field hockey's gameplay and the unique tactics within its wheels. You must make these a part of you and know them like the back of your hand. One of the most technical skills in field hockey is one many do not talk about, 'the offensive side.' People spend a lot of time learning to defend and scale through strikes, but few talk about the technicality of a good offense.

This chapter introduces the offensive strategy, what it entails, and how to make it a part of your hockey strengths. You learn to make good passes from pre-existing patterns proven effective in any game. To wrap it up, you'll discover the basics of a good game strategy in field hockey. Good luck as you uncover the richness of this unique game.

Introduction to Offensive Tactics

Every game has two sides, which consist of the offenders and the defenders. As a player, you may opt for the latter. Many tactics have been dedicated specifically to the defensive games of field hockey, which has left offensive tactics a mystery to many. Therefore, you can use this loophole to your advantage. This section explores the keys that unlock great tactics as an offensive player. Offensive playing is about teamwork. It is the secret to creating openings and opportunities for good and clean shots. The offensive requires strategic and precise movements to gain a score. You must know how to rightly position yourself to stand a chance against the opposing team's defense. Here are some excellent strategies for offensive tactics:

Communication Is Key

Without good communication, there is no good teamwork. You must work closely with your teammates to make a coordinated, well-planned move with good timing and passing. When your communication is good and your team achieves excellent coordination, you can successfully keep the opposing defense always on edge and destabilized. You must apply good dribbling and passing skills to overtake or outmaneuver any defenders.

Good Penetration

Penetration is a great offensive strategy to use to your advantage. It involves advancing into your opponent's shooting circle to create a scoring opportunity successfully.

You can penetrate your opponent's defense line in many ways. For example, when making quick passes, applying good dribbling techniques, and making unpredictable and deceptive moves.

Making a Triangle: A triangle is a good formation where you and other players make a precise and amazing pattern on the field. It gives you an effective pass and other movements of choice. Besides the triangle, you can apply the 'overlap' method. You and the other players take turns to move forward toward the opposing line. It helps maintain tactics and puts pressure on a defense line.

17. Triangle formation in field hockey. Source:
https://www.ahockeyworld.net/wp-content/uploads/triangle-1.jpg

The Offensive tactics require you to be fierce and intentional. It will only be effective when it is planned to use every defense technique possible. Here's an overview of what offense should entail:

- Ensure your eyes are always up and your body is low to the ground.

- Maintain a position between each line, 5 yards to be precise.

- Look up when passing to your partner's stick.

- You must be aggressive.

- If you don't have possession of the ball, create room for your teammates.

- Always keep your stick to the ground.

Creating Passing Patterns and Movements

Taking good passes is an essential skill in field hockey. Familiarizing yourself with as many pass tactics as possible to keep up with a good game is essential. As a beginner, you won't be accustomed to proper passing tactics. Even if you are, you may need to understand how to apply them correctly. You can pass using various techniques such as scooping, hitting, flicking, sweeping, and pushing. Like the dribble techniques, you can create or take advantage of amazing scoring opportunities when players cross the ball or when the ball hits the center of the field, opening opportunities for one lucky player to shoot it into the net. Here are ways to create good passing patterns:

Positioning

Being in the right position before receiving the ball helps identify your opponent's defender and your teammate's positions for good passing. It's about the opening and positioning. You may feel obscured and frustrated when in a situation with no teammates around for your offense and nowhere to make a successful pass. So, keep your eyes up and make calculated decisions before and after receiving the ball.

Read Your Opponent's Defense

Field hockey is similar to chess. Every move must be planned and calculated. It's okay if you find this difficult as a beginner, but you become more skillful after every game because you put your knowledge to work and see things realistically. Every defense has a gap, a loophole you can penetrate and exploit with your passes. Look for them in anticipation and make a quick and effective decision. Timing and accuracy are skills you must master in this game.

Using the Give-and-Go Method

In this technique, you pass the ball to your teammate and move to an angle to receive it back immediately. It's an amazing way to change the point of attack or attention and catch defenders out of position. You must learn to make supporting runs on behalf of your teammates. A well-timed pass can help them continue their run and catch the defense off guard. When you pass ahead, you can create a good attacking opportunity.

Angles and Good Vision: Sometimes, you receive the ball only to have the opposing team's defender snatch it from behind. Place yourself in a position where you can make an approach for the ball and see your teammates and the intended passing position. Maintain a position that gives you a good insight into who is ahead and around you.

By developing your passing skills and understanding the necessity of patterns and movements, you'll become a more skilled and valuable asset to your team's offensive strategies. You must be focused, practice consistently, and measure your ability to create effective passing patterns on the field.

Understanding the Basics of Game Strategy

Each team in field hockey has 11 players. The game aims to move the ball beyond the opponent's defense line and score a goal. Each player can function as an attacker or a defender. The goalkeeper is the team's last line of defense. The best similar sport to field hockey is soccer. The ball is the center of attention, and it's always in motion within the spaces of each team player rather than in direct contact, like in basketball. Here are helpful tips to help you better understand the basics of this unique game:

- A game lasts for one hour, divided into four quarters of 15 minutes each.

- Each team has 11 players on the field.

- The back and side of the goal's net is 18 inches in height.

- Two umpires officiate the matches.

- The ball must always be passed or dribbled with the flat side of your stick, or you will be penalized.

- A goal is scored when a player shoots the ball within the striking circle and into the opposing team's net.

- Goals outside the striking circle will not be counted.

- Your body or stick must shield the ball.

- You have an equal chance to other players to play the ball.

- A hockey stick's weight must not exceed 737g.

For you to fully understand what the striking circle is and the rules that apply to it, you must first be familiar with the field dimension and division.

- Hockey fields are rectangular, with a length of 91.4m and a width of 55m.

- The field is divided in two halves by one centerline. Each half is further divided by 23m and the "D," or striking circle.

- The striking circle is a semi-circle of about 14.6m.

- The goal post is located within the "D".

- The circles are for penalties, which can be a great opportunity for your team to make good scores.

- Goalkeepers arm themselves with padded gloves to protect their hands, chest, and legs, a helmet for the head, and a face mask to protect their face against incoming balls.

Every good game needs a team of skilled players. Field hockey is not an exception. You must be acquainted with many tactics to become an exceptional player. First, you must understand the need for a game plan with good strategies. Understanding a game plan is the key to an offensive play, not for your needs alone, but for a team to effectively plan ahead of every game. Another essential skill is passing tactics. No player can be effective without great passing techniques. Equally, an effective communication system with your teammates and a sharp, keen eye will determine your opponent's defense to find loopholes in every defense triangle and create scoring opportunities for you. The only way to imbibe these techniques is by practicing consistently and diligently. Keep practicing until you develop the mastery you need. Good luck, player.

Chapter 7: Fitness and Conditioning for Field Hockey

Staying fit and maintaining good conditioning in field hockey is key to mastering the game. You must be fierce and explosive on the field to control your game. You must move rapidly and be precise when changing directions to maximize goal-scoring opportunities. As a defender on the field, you should always respond to attacking movements quickly. Imagine how tense and impossible that would be without fitness training. You must engage in specific fitness drills to meet the standard of an average field hockey player. It requires more vigorous movements and drills.

It could have been a bit easier if all you had to do was slide on ice to pass the ball rather than make actual movements with your feet and tense your muscles. However, in field hockey, it's all about agility and endurance, with strong cardiovascular fitness and staying focused until the end of the match. This chapter gives you essential warm-ups and stretching routines before, during, and after every game. You will learn to build endurance and agility, stay injury-free, and apply proper conditioning techniques. It takes more than handling the stick and moving the ball to make shots to be a great field hockey player. You should undergo several drill techniques to keep fit, strong, and swift for a match. Good luck, champion.

Essential Warm-Up and Stretching Routines

Being a beginner in field hockey opens you to several opportunities to read and learn from the mistakes of those in the league. You should know that field hockey can get very demanding and entails various bodily exercises to maintain excellent physical and mental agility. You will be exposed to high-intensity running interspersed with interruptions from other players. It doesn't end there. More running is required until it gets so much you feel your lungs burn. It's okay to feel this way as a beginner. However, you must learn the movements and rapid acceleration and be able to change direction at any time. It sounds daunting, but the good part is you have time to train and learn before venturing into a game. A crucial part of training is thorough warm-up and stretching routines. Below is a breakdown of what this entails:

18. Start your warm-up with a slow run. Source: https://www.pexels.com/photo/selective-focus-photography-of-woman-in-pink-shirt-1199590/

Warm-Ups

Your warm-ups can begin with low-intensity and gradually build from simple and general movements to more specific exercises. Here are some warm-up examples, but you can adjust the specifics to suit your space, time, and other conditions:

- Start with a slow run. Do 2 laps around the field, then include running backward, sideways, lifting your knees, and kicking your heels backward.

- Have 10 minutes of dynamic or static stretching (discussed later).

- Make zigzag runs for 5 counts.

- Work on sprinting with a run length of 5×20m.

- Carry out hockey drills like passing and dribbling.

Goalkeeping Warm-Up

Goalkeeping has its specific fitness routine. Goalkeepers must focus on flexibility and explosive power drills. They have a separate session before a match to test and hone their reflexes. Also, like the players, they must have periods of rest to ease their muscles and joints. This rest period should be done consistently for a safe and active performance.

Stretching Routines

Routine stretches are essential for a field hockey match. As a player, you must take time to minimize muscle imbalance and improve your endurance and field performance. You never know what stretching does for you until you enter a match without doing it. Just like footballers stretch their arms and legs and bend back and forth to ease untapped muscles, you should do the same before training or a game.

When is the best time for stretching?

You carry out stretching routines when you've successfully done a warm-up for 5-10 minutes and feel your muscles warm and relaxed. You can do routine stretches between and after match breaks when playing in a field hockey tournament. Two stretches you can do are dynamic and static.

Rules for Dynamic Stretching

- Start with warm-ups, then stretch your muscles until warm and relaxed.

- Do not fling or throw your body around. Take control of your movements using your muscles.

- As you do, you will feel your muscles slightly resisting. You should not feel pain during a stretch.

- Make slow and intense movements and gradually increase the speed into different ranges of movements for 10-15 minutes.

- Finish with field hockey drills and repeat 8-10 times

Rules for Static Stretching

- Ensure your muscles are warmed and relaxed.

- Take your muscles slowly to the end of their range. You will experience slight resistance but not pain.

- Hold a stretch position and remain static. Don't try to bounce.

- Each stretch should be maintained for 20-30 seconds and repeated 3-4 times.

Building Endurance and Agility

You must possess high endurance to perform at an advanced and elite level. Your training should include long distances and interval distances. Long distances prepare you for playing soundly on the field even after a long time. Short interval training is to help your pushes, passes, dribbling, and scoring. They increase speed and accuracy on the field. Switch between long-distance training and short-interval training to make your workouts lively and fun.

Agility

Agility is a key component of field hockey skills you need to master. It is your ability to respond swiftly and accurately to your body movements. For example, when your teammates pass you a ball during a match, you must be equipped to immediately change direction and control the ball regardless of the pressure. At these times, you must create a path at the last minute and take a shot. The ball is always on the move, and so must you be. With good speed and agility, you can avoid many injuries.

How to Implement Agility Drills

- Form a diamond shape using five cones. Place a cone in the middle.

- Start at the center of your diamond shape.

- Sprint around the cone in front of you in a forward movement. Back-peddle, moving backward to the cone furthest away from you.

- Shuffle sideways to the cone on your left.

- Shuffle back to the furthest cone on your right.

- Return to the middle cone after completing this drill four times.

- Remember to time yourself during this drill to track improvements and speed.

- For additional agility training, carry out this drill while dribbling to make it more practical and game-realistic.

- Be sure to improve on your stick work while you work out.

Staying Injury-Free with Proper Conditioning

Conditioning is necessary for the physical preparation of a game as an athlete. It bridges the gap between your current abilities and what the game demands of you as a player. Also, consider the health standard for players and maintain it throughout your game performance. Why is staying injury-free necessary for field hockey?

Field hockey is built on consistent high-intensity moves like sprinting, shooting, and agility. These moves carry a certain injury risk. If you put your body under high demand when it's not ready, you sign up for future strains and injuries. You cannot give what you don't have. You must have been exposed to vigorous training to withstand pressure during a match. One common injury in field hockey is a sprain. This happens when you haven't increased the capacity of your muscles to stabilize your ankles or wrists.

Causes of Injuries in Field Hockey

- High impact or collision with other players.
- Impact with a goalpost.
- Hockey sticks.
- Moving at high speed with the ball.

- Shoe studs.

Tips to Prevent Injuries

- Make sure you warm up before a game or training.
- Stretch your hips, groins, and lower back.
- Wear protective gear, especially for a beginner.
- Know and abide by the rules of the game.
- Maintain proper rest and keep hydrated
- Off-season training builds body strength and flexibility.

Field hockey transforms into a lifestyle for every player. As much as it is fun and interesting, certain skills and fitness levels must be met to qualify as a player. You must be flexible, fast, and sharp, with good agility and endurance, ready for your games. You need good conditioning and training to avoid injuries. Always carry out warm-ups, stretches, and other field hockey drills to keep improving. You must improve your footwork and stick work and develop a system to preserve energy reserves.

Chapter 8: Goalkeeping Basics for Beginners

In the exhilarating world of field hockey, goalkeepers hold a vital role that can often determine the outcome of a match. This chapter is tailored to beginners stepping into the goalkeeper's shoes for the first time. It introduces you to the core concepts forming the bedrock of successful goalkeeping and delves into specifics. However, before delving into specifics, here's a brief overview of the key elements.

As a beginner goalkeeper, it's essential to acquaint yourself with the necessary equipment to ensure your safety and performance on the field. This chapter introduces the primary gear, including goalkeeper pads, gloves, kickers, helmets, and protective clothing. Each piece has a unique purpose to safeguard you against hard shots and collisions, allowing you to focus on your technique and skill.

Positioning is the cornerstone of effective goalkeeping in field hockey. How you stand and position yourself greatly influences your ability to defend against shots. The basics of your stance, including how to set your feet, position your body, and hold your hands, are explained. Understanding the angles relative to the goalposts is vital to cutting down the attacking player's options and maximizing your chances of stopping shots.

Blocking shots and making saves is where the magic of goalkeeping truly happens. A glimpse into the various techniques and strategies for thwarting the opponent's attempts is covered, and you will gain insights into different saves, such as kick, stick, and pad saves. This chapter touches upon hand-eye coordination, positioning, and staying sufficiently focused to react swiftly to unpredictable shots.

As you progress through this chapter, each element will be explored in depth, equipping you with the knowledge and skills necessary to excel as a field hockey goalkeeper. So, step onto the field, break down these components, and lay the groundwork for your journey toward becoming a formidable presence between the posts.

Introduction to Goalkeeping Equipment

In the exhilarating sport of field hockey, goalkeepers are the last line of defense tasked with thwarting an opponent's attempt to score. Goalkeepers rely on specialized equipment for protection, enhanced performance, and agile movement to perform this critical role effectively. This section introduces you to the essential goalkeeping gear, ensuring your safety and empowering you to excel on the field.

Goalkeeper Pads

Goalkeeper pads are a goalkeeper's primary line of defense against high-speed shots. These leg guards provide ample coverage for your lower limbs, from the shin down to the upper foot. They absorb impact and redirect the ball away from the goal. Goalkeeper pads offer protection and rebound control.

Goalkeeper Gloves

Goalkeeper gloves are your most crucial tool for securing the ball and making saves. These gloves offer enhanced grip and protection for your hands and fingers. The padded palms and fingers help cushion the impact of hard shots, providing you with the dexterity to control the ball.

Kickers

Kickers are worn on the goalkeeper's feet and play a pivotal role in blocking shots. These protective foot-guards have a broad, flat surface to deflect shots away from the goal. Kickers enable goalkeepers to use their feet to make saves while keeping their legs and feet well protected.

Helmet and Face Protector

Safety is paramount. A helmet with a face protector shields the goalkeeper's head and face from potential injury. The face protector ensures your vision remains unobstructed while protecting against high-speed shots and collisions.

Body Armor

Body armor adds an extra layer of protection to your chest, abdomen, and other vulnerable areas. It helps minimize the impact of shots and collisions, allowing you to focus on your positioning and technique without fearing injury.

Specialized Footwear

Field hockey goalkeeper shoes provide the necessary grip and support on the field. The cleats on these shoes offer traction, enabling goalkeepers to move quickly and maintain stability during dives and saves.

As you delve into your goalkeeping journey, each piece of equipment has a distinct purpose to enhance your performance and ensure your safety. By understanding and using your gear effectively, you are better equipped to defend your goal and make crucial saves during intense matches.

Goalkeeping Stance and Positioning

A solid stance and impeccable positioning are the cornerstones of effective goalkeeping in field hockey. As the last line of defense, your stance determines your readiness to react to shots and your ability to cut down shooting angles. This section explains the critical aspects of goalkeeping stance and positioning, empowering you to command the goal confidently.

Balanced Stance

19. Balanced stance. Source: https://www.ahockeyworld.net/wp-content/uploads/c.jpg

Begin with a balanced stance, evenly distributing your weight on both feet. This stance allows you to move quickly in any direction and react swiftly to incoming shots. Avoid favoring one leg over the other, as it can limit mobility.

Feet Positioning

Position your feet shoulder-width apart, maintaining a slight bend at the knees. Your feet should be parallel to the goal line, with your toes pointing slightly outward. This stance provides stability and ensures you're prepared to cover both sides of the goal.

Body Alignment

Align your body with the center of the goal. Your chest, hips, and shoulders should face the direction of play. This alignment minimizes gaps between your body and the goalposts, making it challenging for opponents to find openings to shoot through.

Hand Placement

Hold your hands in front of your body, slightly away from your chest. Your hands should be open and relaxed, ready to move and react. Keep your palms facing the field to maximize coverage and control.

Anticipation and Readiness

Constantly assess the game and anticipate the players and the ball's movements. Stay on the balls of your feet to enable quick movement. Be ready to adjust your stance based on the ball's position and the angle of attack.

Angles and Positioning

Understanding angles is paramount. Position yourself closer to the near post when the ball is on that side of the field. Adjust your positioning to cover potential shooting angles effectively as the ball shifts to the center or opposite side.

Goal Line Awareness

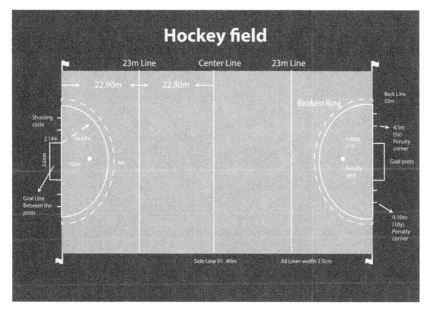

20. The goal line is the line in between the posts. Source:
https://i.ytimg.com/vi/MViNYpd68sg/maxresdefault.jpg

Maintain awareness of your distance from the goal line. Avoid straying too far from the goal, leaving you vulnerable to chip shots or quick passes. Balance being proactive in cutting down angles with the need to protect your goal line.

Mastering your stance and positioning as a field hockey goalkeeper lays the foundation for your success. You'll be better equipped to read the game, react swiftly to shots, and confidently command your territory between the posts by consistently practicing and refining these techniques.

Blocking Shots and Making Saves

The heart of a field hockey goalkeeper's role lies in blocking shots and remarkable saves. Developing these skills requires a blend of technique, timing, and anticipation. The techniques and strategies allowing you to stand as a formidable barrier against opponents' attempts to score are covered below.

Diving Saves

21. Diving saves are effective at denying your opponent's shots. Source: https://www.rachaellynch.com.au/wp-content/uploads/2011/08/Goalie_Dive_2.jpg

Diving saves are dramatic and effective at denying your opponent's shots. Push off with your back foot to execute a successful dive and extend your body toward the ball. Keep your eyes on the ball and use your gloves and pads to deflect or trap the shot. Proper technique minimizes the risk of injury and maximizes your chances of making a save.

Stick Saves

22. *Stick saves involve using your stick to block a shot. Source: https://i.ytimg.com/vi/75pF47oJvuA/maxresdefault.jpg*

Using your stick to block shots is a crucial skill. Position your stick horizontally in front of you, parallel to the ground. React quickly by extending your stick to intercept shots aimed low or along the ground. Your stick's length gives additional reach, making it a valuable tool for saves.

Pad Saves

Your goalkeeper pads help block shots while minimizing rebounds. Angle your pads to redirect shots away from the goal. For shots aimed at the lower portion of the goal, drop your leading leg and angle your pad downward to create a barrier that the ball will bounce off.

Quick Reactions

Reacting swiftly to unexpected shots requires sharp reflexes. Keep your eyes on the ball and track its movement closely. It helps you predict the trajectory and respond faster to shots, enabling you to make saves even in fast-paced situations.

Smothering Loose Balls

When the ball is loose in front of the goal, smothering it prevents opponents from capitalizing on rebounds. Drop to your knees and cover the ball with your body, using your gloves and pads to secure it. This technique prevents attackers from getting a clear shot at the goal.

Communication

Effective communication with your teammates is essential. Alert defenders to opponents' movements and coordinate your actions to prevent attackers from getting into advantageous positions. Good communication enhances anticipating shots and responding effectively.

Mental Focus

Maintain unwavering concentration throughout the game. Stay engaged, even during inactive periods, as a sudden shot can come at any moment. Mental focus enhances reading the game, anticipating shots, and reacting swiftly.

You'll evolve into a reliable and skilled field hockey goalkeeper by honing these blocking and saving techniques. Practice, repetition, and a commitment to improving your skills will elevate your game, enabling you to make match-defining saves and turn the tide in your team's favor.

Chapter 9: Rules and Officiating in Field Hockey

Field hockey is a dynamic and exhilarating sport hinging on carefully structured rules and regulations. These rules govern every aspect of play, ensuring fairness, safety, and a level playing field for both teams. This chapter gives an overview of the fundamental rules and the crucial role of officials while enforcing them. Understanding these rules is essential for players, coaches, and spectators as they shape the game's flow and outcome.

The Framework of Rules

Field hockey is played within a well-defined framework of rules established by the International Hockey Federation (FIH). These rules outline the field's dimensions, the match duration, the number of players on each team, and other essential parameters. A solid grasp of these foundational rules is essential for anyone participating in or watching the game.

Objectives and Play

The objective of field hockey is simple: to score goals while preventing the opposing team from doing the same. Players use their sticks to pass the ball, dribble, and shoot. Passing and movement are integral to advancing the ball strategically and creating scoring opportunities.

Officiating and Officials

Field hockey matches are overseen by officials who are there to ensure the game is played with integrity and according to the rules. The officiating team typically consists of two umpires. These officials enforce the rules, decide on fouls, award penalties, and maintain order on the field.

Fouls and Penalties

Field hockey has specific guidelines for legal and illegal actions. Fouls, such as obstructing an opponent, using the body to intentionally block the ball, or making dangerous plays, result in penalties for the opposing team. Depending on the severity and location of the foul, the team will be awarded a free hit, a penalty corner, or a penalty stroke.

Sportsmanship and Fair Play

Respect for the rules and sportsmanship are integral to the spirit of field hockey. Players are expected to uphold fair play, respect opponents and officials, and play the game with sportsmanship. Unsportsmanlike conduct, like arguing with officials or intentionally violating rules, can result in penalties for the player or team or disqualification.

23. Avoid unsportsmanlike conduct when playing field hockey. Source: https://unsplash.com/photos/SwnOYOy6mbM?utm_source=unsplash&utm_medium=referral&utm_content=creditShareLink

Understanding the rules and the officials' roles enhances your enjoyment of field hockey and contributes to the game's overall quality. Whether a player, coach, or spectator, a solid understanding of these fundamental aspects allows you to engage with the sport on a deeper level, appreciate the strategy and skill involved, and celebrate the moments of excitement field hockey brings to the fore.

Understanding Common Game Violations

Field hockey is governed by rules to ensure fair play, safety, and smooth progression. Violations of these rules, known as fouls, can lead to penalties for the offending team. As a player, coach, or spectator, clearly understanding these game violations is crucial to fully appreciate the dynamics of field hockey. This section explores some of the most frequently encountered fouls and their implications.

Obstruction

Obstruction occurs when a player uses their body or stick to prevent an opponent from playing the ball. It includes shielding the ball with the body, placing the stick between the opponent and the ball, or backing into an opponent. The player with the ball must allow the opponent to tackle or challenge for the ball. The result is a free hit awarded to the non-offending team.

Dangerous Play

Dangerous play refers to actions posing a risk to the safety of players. Examples include raising the stick above the waist, swinging the stick recklessly, or playing the ball dangerously close to another player's body. Dangerous play can result in a free hit or penalty, depending on the severity and the action's intent.

Backstick

Using the stick's rounded side (the back) to play the ball is considered a violation known as a backstick. Players must use the stick's flat side (forehand) to hit, control, or pass the ball. A free hit is awarded to the opposing team if a player is caught using the back of the stick.

Foot or Body Contact

Players are not allowed to intentionally use their feet, legs, or any part of their body to play the ball. However, accidental contact is sometimes permissible, and an advantage is awarded. If a player uses their body to intentionally stop or redirect the ball, the opposing team is awarded a free hit.

Lifted Ball

Hitting a ball so it rises off the ground to a dangerous height is considered a lifted ball. If the lifted ball threatens players' safety, play is stopped, and the opposing team is awarded a free hit from where the dangerous play occurred.

Overhead (Aerial) Passes

While overhead passes can be spectacular, they must be executed carefully. An overhead pass above shoulder height that lands within the opponent's defensive 23-meter area can result in a turnover of possession.

Understanding and recognizing these common violations enhances your ability to follow the game's progression and appreciate the officials' decisions. As players strive to master the nuances of field hockey, umpires are crucial to enforcing the rules and ensuring the game is played fairly and safely.

Roles of Umpires

Umpires are the guardians of fairness and order in field hockey. Their presence ensures matches are played within the rules' boundaries, ensuring the sport's integrity and safety. Here's an exploration of the critical responsibilities these officials shoulder:

Rule Enforcement

They enforce field hockey's rules, diligently monitoring players' actions to prevent violations and fouls. Their unwavering commitment to upholding the rules creates a level playing field for all teams to have an equal chance to succeed.

Decision Making

In the heat of the match, umpires make instantaneous decisions on fouls, penalties, and other critical aspects. Their swift and accurate judgments impact the course of the game, ensuring players adhere to the rules and compete fairly.

Positioning and Movement

Strategic positioning is paramount for umpires. Their placement on the field allows them to effectively observe the action, anticipate potential rule violations, and make informed decisions. Their positioning augments the game's flow.

Communication

Effective communication is the cornerstone of successful officiating. Umpires communicate with players, coaches, and each other to clarify decisions, give warnings, and maintain open lines of dialogue throughout the match.

Penalty Decisions

Determining appropriate penalties for infractions falls under the purview of umpires. Based on the severity and context of the foul, they apply penalties such as free hits, penalty corners, or penalty strokes. Their decisions reflect a thorough understanding of the game's rules.

Player Safety

Umpires prioritize player safety above all else. They monitor the field for dangerous play and unsportsmanlike conduct, intervening when necessary to prevent potential harm and maintain a safe environment for all players.

Maintaining Match Flow

Umpires contribute to the ebb and flow of the game, managing stoppages and restarts to ensure a seamless match experience. Their adept management of the match's pace keeps players engaged and spectators enthralled.

In essence, umpires embody sportsmanship and fairness in field hockey. Their watchful eyes and decisive actions ensure the spirit of the game is upheld, allowing players to showcase their skills and passion on a stage governed by honesty. As participants and enthusiasts, understanding and respecting these officials' roles elevates the enjoyment and appreciation of field hockey.

Fair Play and Respect in the Game

Field hockey is a display of skill and athleticism and a platform for embracing the values of fair play and respect. These core principles underpin the sport's essence, creating an environment where players, coaches, officials, and spectators come together to celebrate the beauty of competition. This section delves into the significance of fair play and respect in field hockey.

Fair Play

Fair play is the foundation upon which field hockey was built. It emphasizes integrity, honesty, and adherence to the rules. Players are expected to compete with a genuine desire to win while respecting the rights of opponents to do the same. It includes accepting the officials' decisions, acknowledging opponents' successes, and refraining from unsportsmanlike conduct.

Sportsmanship

Sportsmanship embodies the spirit of fair play. It encompasses treating opponents, teammates, officials, and fans respectfully and courteously. Players are encouraged to show grace in victory and resilience in defeat. Good sportsmanship fosters a positive atmosphere and promotes camaraderie among all involved.

Respect for Officials

Respect for officials is paramount. Their decisions shape the game, and players' attitudes toward them influence the match's overall dynamics. Players should communicate with officials respectfully, accept their judgments, and refrain from questioning or disputing decisions aggressively.

Respect for Opponents

Vigorously competing does not preclude treating opponents with respect. Players should avoid intentional or excessive physical contact, taunting, or trash talk undermining the game's spirit. Treating opponents fairly and acknowledging their efforts contributes to a healthy and enjoyable competitive atmosphere.

Safety and Fairness

Respecting the safety of fellow players is a fundamental aspect of fair play. Actions endangering opponents through dangerous plays or reckless behavior undermine the sport's principles. Upholding safety standards ensures the game remains a platform for showcasing skill without compromising well-being.

Upholding the Image of the Sport

Players, coaches, and officials have a role in upholding the image of field hockey. By embodying fair play and respect, they contribute to the positive perception of the sport in the eyes of fans, communities, and the larger sporting world.

Leading by Example

Players at all levels can inspire the next generation by embracing fair play and respect. Young athletes learn from their role models, and demonstrating these values on and off the field shapes their understanding of sportsmanship.

In the vibrant tapestry of field hockey, fair play and respect are the threads weaving together the rich experiences of athletes, coaches, and spectators. They transcend wins and losses, embodying sportsmanship ideals enriching the game's legacy. Participants elevate the collective experience of field hockey and leave a lasting impact on the sport's culture by embracing these values.

Chapter 10: Growing as a Field Hockey Player

Now that you know everything about field hockey, you may be raring to try your hand at it. Build a team and give it a go. If you have already played the game and loved it, you could be wondering where you can go from there. You can keep playing as you have been, of course. However, wouldn't it be better to learn new skills, discover more strategies, and grow as a field hockey player?

24. Continuing to practice these skills will help you develop as a field hockey player. Source:
https://unsplash.com/photos/fQgWu6vamvY?utm_source=unsplash&utm_medium=referral&utm_content=creditShareLink

The information in this book is comprehensive and perfect for navigating field hockey, but this is just the tip of a fathomless iceberg. When you have found your footing, there's no better way to experience everything this game offers than by playing it over and over again.

You don't always need a full team to play. Try mini-hockey with three or more players on each side on a smaller field. Can't find anyone to play with? Don't hesitate to practice by yourself. Here are a few advanced practice tips to become a better field hockey player.

Advanced Practice Tips

- ### Sprint Workout

Undoubtedly, endurance is important for field hockey. You must be constantly on the move on a 1.24-acre ground. Did you know that your sprinting skills could make or break the game? You cannot expect to go from zero to your maximum running speed in under a second. Even experienced sprinters like Usain Bolt cannot do that.

But you don't want to take too much time either. You never know when or how long to sprint to collect a long pass. Heed these tips to help increase your sprint velocity.

1. Maintain good form while sprinting. Speed is mostly about the aerodynamics of an object. Also, proper posture imbues balance in your body, so you fall less while sprinting. Keep your back straight and bend a little forward at the waist.

2. Avoid touching your heels on the ground when sprinting. When you run only on the balls of your feet, you get more acceleration and longer strides.

3. Ensure your arms face the direction in which you are sprinting. Don't move them across your chest. It will hinder your aerodynamics.

4. Practice running barefoot. It will make your feet stronger so you can sprint faster.

- **Improve Your Footwork**

As you know, touching the ball with your foot is penalized in field hockey. Even if accidental, it can result in a free hit for the opposition. Since your feet are often close to the ball while handling it with the stick, it is sometimes difficult to avoid contact. Focus on your footwork. Place your feet away from the ball's direction. Gain perfect control over your lower body and maintain overall balance using these tips.

1. **Athleticism Is the Key**. The more athletic you are, the better your footwork will be. Practice box jumping, step climbing, glute-ham raises, squats, etc. Get your feet ready to take the strain of a 60-minute game.

2. **Balance Is Vital to Your Footwork**. Take up yoga to increase your balance and maintain a good body posture. Alternatively, you can practice these exercises - single leg balance, single leg squat, leg swings, or ride your bike on uneven terrain for an hour or two.

3. **Hold the Ball in Your Hockey Stick's Heel and Run Straight**. Take a sharp turn midway, keeping the ball in the heel. The side strafe or shuffle you commit to during the turn improves your footwork.

- **Practice Your Passing and Receiving**

Field hockey is a team game, so passing the ball is critical to winning a game. The more accurate your passes, the better your team's possession, and the higher your team's chances of scoring goals. Practice quick short passes followed by long grip hits. Hit a cone at longer distances, even from one corner of the field to the other.

Receiving the ball is as important as passing it. If you cannot properly collect the ball onto your stick, then the accurate pass made by your teammate will be worthless. No matter how hard the pass, you should receive the ball without letting it bounce or deflect too far from your stick. Here are two passing and receiving drills you can practice.

1. Two-player passing drills include square passing (moving the ball back and forth between you as you run left and right parallel to each other), cross-over passing (when you let your teammate take the ball while you're dribbling your way across the field), and strategic passing (based on your strategy for the game).

2. Three-player passing might seem easy at first sight, but it requires excellent coordination between the players. Each player stands on three points of an imaginary triangle, one in the front and two on defense. Keep passing the ball to each other as you slowly move forward. Maintain the triangle's shape as much as possible.

- **Dribble Like a Pro**

Hockey is primarily a team game, but there have been several instances when a single player has managed to turn the match around. They are usually top-class dribblers with exceptional ball control. You, too, can dribble like a pro if you practice these steps every day.

1. Start with the standard hockey stance with your knees bent and hands gripping the stick in front of you.

2. Keep the ball just ahead of you so you can comfortably reach it with the stick without breaking your stance.

3. Tap the ball from side to side with the flat face of the stick. You will flip the stick each time to connect its flat part with the ball.

4. Once you get into the groove of dribbling, move slowly forward. With each tap of the ball, push it ahead at an angle.

You can learn better control with air dribbling. Scoop the ball up on your stick's flat face and tap it from one side to the other like a semicircular juggle, hitting with the flat face each time.

Setting Goals and Tracking Progress

It is crucial to set goals for the tasks you undertake. It is even more so for field hockey. Your training regime and drills' intensity will vary depending on your goals. Ask yourself one important question. Why do you want to play field hockey? Do you want to participate in a championship or use the game to build fitness? Or do you want to play the game just for the sake of it?

According to your goals, you must keep track of your progress. Make a daily note of the drills and exercises you performed, the strategies you implemented, and the hours you practiced. Track your progress each week or month, and keep pushing your goals' boundaries.

Embracing Sportsmanship and Teamwork

Field hockey is exciting and enjoyable to play if everyone follows the rules. So, don't break the rules and ruin the game for the other players. However, adherence to the rules and regulations is only one part of sportsmanship.

To embrace the spirit of the game completely, you must encourage your teammates and respect your opponents. Always be at the top of your game, even if your opposition is weak. Listen to the umpires and respect their decisions. Even if you feel they are wrong, don't lose your cool. State your opinions politely. Remember, the umpires are also human and can make mistakes sometimes.

Field hockey is a team game. Rarely, if ever, can one player change the fate of the entire team on their own. Even if you are a top-notch player, you need your team to make a commendable impact on the sport. So, always ensure to work as a team. Your sudden burst of speed and display of skills from defense to the offensive line will be of no avail if your teammates are left behind and you have nobody to pass the ball to.

Make even the least skillful player in your team feel valued. Help them unlock their potential. Listen to what the more experienced players say, but don't hesitate to speak your mind if you feel they have strayed. Your teamwork will be tested willy-nilly on the field during a game, so you learn to make split-second decisions to benefit your team, not just yourself.

Conclusion

Field hockey is one of the best field games in the world, and luckily, by reading this book, you've realized it is not as complex as initially considered. You discovered the game's fundamental rules and were provided with a clear understanding of its gameplay and powerful techniques. This guide cuts across several basics and advances of field hockey, from mastering ball control, learning dribbling techniques, maneuvering the ball through your opponent's defenses, and shooting and scoring techniques, exposing you to shooting at different lengths and positions. It guides you in applying great defensive strategies as a beginner and equips you with the necessary knowledge to play and become a pivotal role among your teammates.

The next step is to carry out everything you've understood and learned. To become a master of field hockey techniques, you must apply the principles discussed in each chapter. Practice is the key to improvement. Dedicate time to practicing stick work, ball control, strikes, and goalkeeping skills. Join the local club or league and practice to gain experience and exposure to games. Apply different playing styles and see which works best. Do not try to do it all at once, as you could get overwhelmed. Start with one technique and practice until you gain mastery, then move on to others.

It would be wonderful to get your feedback. Share your experience, journey, challenges, and lessons learned when applying the various techniques. Your reviews will go a long way toward inspiring others on this amazing journey of field hockey mastery. Pursuing your dreams, remember that field hockey is more than a sport. It's a lifestyle that shapes character and resilience, builds friendship, and fuels passion. Get your kit and hit the field running. Make every moment count.

References

(N.d.). Compuwarehockey.org. https://www.compuwarehockey.org/page/show/5145091-usa-hockey-declaration-of-player-safety-fair-play-and-respect

(N.d.). Masterclass.com. https://www.masterclass.com/articles/how-to-sprint-faster

(N.d.). Ussportscamps.com. https://www.ussportscamps.com/tips/fieldhockey/field-hockey-drills-to-improve-agilityhttps://www.ussportscamps.com/tips/fieldhockey/field-hockey-drills-to-improve-agility

(N.d.-a). Djfh.org. https://www.djfh.org/fh101#:~:text=The%20best%20way%20to%20describe,than%20directly%20to%20a%20teammate

(N.d.-a). Fieldhockeybc.com. https://fieldhockeybc.com/wp-content/uploads/2016/11/GOALKEEPINGFUNDAMENTALS_May07.pdf

(N.d.-a). Silverskatefestival.org. https://www.silverskatefestival.org/how-to-dribble-a-field-hockey-ball-the-ultimate-guide/#:~:text=The%20key%20is%20to%20keep,that%20all%20players%20should%20master.

(N.d.-a). Silverskatefestival.org. https://www.silverskatefestival.org/how-to-score-a-field-hockey-goal/

(N.d.-a). Ussportscamps.com. https://www.ussportscamps.com/tips/fieldhockey/how-to-guide-defense-field-hockey

(N.d.-b). Silverskatefestival.org. https://www.silverskatefestival.org/5-tips-to-improve-your-field-hockey-goalie-skills/

(N.d.-b). Ussportscamps.com. https://www.ussportscamps.com/tips/fieldhockey/field-hockey-drill-agility-and-ball-control

(N.d.-b). Ussportscamps.com. https://www.ussportscamps.com/tips/fieldhockey/5-important-skills-for-field-hockey-beginners

(N.d.-b). Ussportscamps.com. https://www.ussportscamps.com/tips/fieldhockey/5-tips-to-be-a-better-field-hockey-goalkeeper

(N.d.-b). Ussportscamps.com. https://www.ussportscamps.com/tips/fieldhockey/basic-field-hockey-terminology

3 ways to play great hockey defense. (2017, February 16). Crossicehockey.com; Digital Media Publications, Inc. https://www.crossicehockey.com/playing-great-hockey-defense/

4 ways field hockey coaches can encourage overall teamwork. (2019, March 4). Revolution Field Hockey Camps. https://www.fhcamps.com/4-ways-field-hockey-coaches-can-encourage-teamwork/

5 Important Skills for Field Hockey Beginners. (n.d.). Ussportscamps.com. https://www.ussportscamps.com/tips/fieldhockey/5-important-skills-for-field-hockey-beginners

Ansari, A. (2022, January 26). Field hockey rules: A guide to understanding the sport. International Olympic Committee. https://olympics.com/en/news/field-hockey-rules-how-to-play

Ansari, A. (2022, January 26). Field hockey rules: A guide to understanding the sport. International Olympic Committee. https://olympics.com/en/news/field-hockey-rules-how-to-play

Coaching tips: Dynamic Stretching. (n.d.). Fieldhockeysticksusa.com. https://www.fieldhockeysticksusa.com/coaching-tips-dynamic-stretching

Davies, H. (2019, March 12). Strength and conditioning for field hockey. Integrate Sports. https://www.integratesports.com/blogs/hockey/strength-and-conditioning

Eddie. (2021, February 27). Five Ways of Hitting a Field Hockey ball. Hockey Hooked. https://hockeyhooked.com/five-ways-of-hitting-a-field-hockey-ball/

Eddie. (2023, July 28). How to dribble in field hockey. Hockey Hooked. https://hockeyhooked.com/how-to-dribble-in-field-hockey/

Eddie. (2023, July 28). How to dribble in field hockey. Hockey Hooked. https://hockeyhooked.com/how-to-dribble-in-field-hockey/

Falla, A. (2006, October 17). How to be a better field hockey player. WikiHow. https://www.wikihow.com/Be-a-Better-Field-Hockey-Player

Field hockey (fall) / basic field hockey rules. (n.d.). K12.Nj.Us. https://www.voorhees.k12.nj.us/Page/32621

Field hockey umpires and officials. (n.d.). Longstreth Sporting Goods. https://longstreth.com/pages/field-hockey-umpires

Field hockey warm-ups. (n.d.). Topendsports.com. https://www.topendsports.com/sport/hockey/warm-up.htm

Goaltenders: Blocking vs. Reacting saves. (2016, February 4). Crossicehockey.com; Digital Media Publications, Inc. https://www.crossicehockey.com/goaltenders-blocking-vs-reacting-saves/

Goaltenders: Blocking vs. Reacting saves. (2016, February 4). Crossicehockey.com; Digital Media Publications, Inc. https://www.crossicehockey.com/goaltenders-blocking-vs-reacting-saves/

Grundy, J. (n.d.). Footwork field hockey drills, videos and coaching plans. Www.sportplan.net. https://www.sportplan.net/s/Hockey/footwork.jsp

Henshaw, A. (2021, October 11). Tackle. Sportslingo.com; SportsLingo. https://www.sportslingo.com/sports-glossary/t/tackle-field-hockey/

Hockey dribbling technique. (n.d.). BBC.
https://www.bbc.co.uk/bitesize/guides/zqm7xsg/revision/5

Hockey drills Passing & receiving coaching skills. (n.d.).
Www.sportplan.net. https://www.sportplan.net/drills/Hockey/Passing-
Receiving/practiceIndex.jsp

Hollis, L. (2016, March 10). Confidence on the hockey pitch. Pure
Hockey.
https://playbetterfieldhockey.wordpress.com/2016/03/10/confidence-
on-the-hockey-pitch/

How to shoot in hockey. (n.d.). Gov.Sg.
https://www.activesgcircle.gov.sg/learn/hockey/how-to-shoot-in-hockey

Jagday, C. S. (2016, July 14). Goal settings for hockey players by Shiv
Jagday. A Hockey World. https://www.ahockeyworld.net/goal-settings-
for-hockey-players-by-shiv-jagday/

longstrethsports. (2016, April 11). Field hockey goalkeeping essentials
list. Longstreth Sports.
https://longstrethsports.wordpress.com/2016/04/11/field-hockey-
goalkeeping-essentials-list/

Marking. (2021, March 20). Hockey Training.
https://www.hockeytraining.co.uk/marking/

Mendoza, P. (2022, May 31). Hockey Goalkeeping: How to teach the
basic stance? A Hockey World. https://www.ahockeyworld.net/hockey-
goalkeeping-teach-basic-stance/

Noticed Collaborator. (2021, January 17). Field hockey equipment list. SV
SPORTS. https://www.svsports.com/blogs/resources/field-hockey-
equipment-list

Penny, L. (2015, August 15). Top up your field hockey tactics. Hockey
Performance Academy. https://hockeyperformanceacademy.com/top-
up-your-field-hockey-tactics/

Penny, L. (2015, February 2). Top 10 field hockey skills to master.
Hockey Performance Academy.
https://hockeyperformanceacademy.com/top-10-field-hockey-skills-to-
master/

Southworth, G. (2021, December 12). How to hold a field hockey stick.
OutdoorTroop. https://outdoortroop.com/how-to-hold-a-field-hockey-
stick/

STICK BASICS. (n.d.). FIELD HOCKEY BASICS. Demosphere-secure.com. https://prod-assets.demosphere-secure.com/_deimos/_public_files/0673xzskkj74b/field-hockey/Field%20Hockey%20Basics%20v2.pdf?CacheKey=1496161448

Stretching guide for field hockey. (n.d.). Barclayphysicaltherapy.com. https://www.barclayphysicaltherapy.com/Sports-Activities/Field-Hockey/Stretching-Guide-for-Field-Hockey/a~4971/article.html

Super User. (n.d.). Field hockey rules. Rulesofsport.com. https://www.rulesofsport.com/sports/hockey-field.html

Super User. (n.d.). Field hockey rules. Rulesofsport.com. https://www.rulesofsport.com/sports/hockey-field.html

The School Of Sports [@TheSchoolOfSports]. (2022, January 23). Hockey Rules✓ Rules of Hockey ✓ Field Hockey. Youtube. https://www.youtube.com/watch?v=M83C70ILng0

What are the five types of fouls in field hockey? (n.d.). Stickhandling PRO. https://www.stickhandlingpro.com/blog/What-Are-the-Five-Types-of-Fouls-in-Field-Hockey/

Wilton, M. (2022, May 10). Defensive strategies and tips for field hockey. SMW. https://www.sm-worldwide.com/post/defensive-strategies-and-tips-for-field-hockey

Printed in Great Britain
by Amazon